All Year Long

poems by

Elaine Day

Published by Feather Books
PO Box 438
Shrewsbury SY3 0WN, UK
Tel/fax; 01743 872177

Website URL: http://www.waddysweb.freeuk.com
e-mail:

GW00692220

No. 257 in the Feather Books Poetry Series

ISBN-10:   1-84175-247-9
ISBN-13:   978-1-84175-247-1

CONTENTS

New Britain

The ever-changing country,
The ever-changing people,
The weather also changes
As we head towards global warming.
The murders seem so often,
The innocence of lives taken,
The young seem to be the victims
Of such an early death.
Elderly are preyed on
For the money that they have,
Maybe just their pensions.
Not a care in the world,
Oh, this is New Britain
With no-one really caring.
Families that seem torn apart.
Marriages that never exist.
Children come now from sperm banks
Not from a mother's womb.
Fathers may never see their children
In this shameful world.
We hope and pray that life will change;
That people one day may care
And love once again their neighbour.

A Crime was Committed

There was a hush in the air
As he walked through the house,
It was cold and damp outside;
Chilly, with a sting of cold breath in.
He trod carefully
pushing back every door
Until he found her
Naked, in the shower.
He stabbed her, twenty times.
She never screamed
But slipped to the ground
In her pool of blood.
A knife was at the door.
He ran. She died.
The police were baffled
As to why.
She was only young
And had a lot to live for.
She never wanted to die
But commit a sin, she never did.
He was never arrested
But ran from the police
Overseas, to a better place
To escape the cold air
Into a warm climate
That was beyond the police

Here in England.
Years later, he died
Overseas, in a pool of blood.
Was it revenge from the grave,
As he was stabbed
Twenty times in the heart?
No one ever knew
But revenge was sought
And justice was done.
The end had come
For the killer was dead.

It's a Happy Day

It's a happy day:
Jesus is raised
From the tomb of the dead
To the land of the living.
I praise him, thank him
For being just him.
Jesus, man of men,
Life is whole each day
It's a happy day.
Jesus is raised.

Autumn Skies

Now that the winter is drawing near
The skies are cloudy, dull, and drawn;
The sun comes up, not very strong;
Leaves fall from the trees
All crisp and golden brown;
Squirrels munch on their nuts,
Birds re-build their nests,
As strong winds take them.
Summer is no longer with us;
So, it is dress up warm
For the winter chills.
Heating goes on around this land.
Colds prevail, days off work
Christmas is such a joy
When turkey is eaten with great gusto.
Drinks are merry, so is the talk.
Snow may fall on our windows
While we stay warm inside.

Profit and Power

If I were famous
And not a mere mortal,
I would be rich,
Not very thin
And sleep around in doors;
But, as I am a mortal
Who's used to anything,
I'm glad of a free lunch
Tea or coffee.
Money comes in slowly
As I write away,
But it is only a dream
As people take your hard-earned money
And spend it on themselves for profit
As yours dwindles away.
Life goes on anyway
As every day's a struggle.
I stay up late,
Arise early, to start again
But, for what I ask
As life goes on
Tomorrow is another day;
Maybe poor, maybe rich,
As I sleep around in doors.

British Injustice

We were once called 'Great,'
Now it's nothing at all,
For now we cave in to Asylum Seekers
Who come over,
Take our jobs
And the Government money.
Our house prices soar
As British cannot afford,
But the man from overseas can;
And the injustice is done.
They take over our shops
And take over our medication.
Where will it all end?
In this country
We called 'Great'
We are just a 'soft touch'
As more and more come in.
Our country is now crowded
With people from overseas
As the English depart
For warmer climates.
Let's have Britain the way it was:
Decent health and houses,
Not shoeboxes one by one
There's nothing healthy about.

England?
No, British injustice is done.

Oh, Give Thanks to The Lord

Oh, give thanks to the Lord
For he is good,
He is your salvation,
Your rising after death.
The Lord is a tower of strength,
Joy and deliverance.
I shall not die, but live
In the home of the Lord above.
So, to the gate of the Lord I go,
The stone that the women rolled back
To reveal the Lord had risen
To heaven up above.

I Saw You Standing There

You died and left the Earth
A broken heart, a failing heart
You knew me well.
I was only five
When you went to heaven
And died.
Your Ghost came back.
You smiled at me.
You whispered, 'Goodbye'
I don't know why,
But God now has you
And I'm left to die.

My heart is sad
For I am lost;
I'm older now.
Soon I'll die.
I'll meet you soon
In God's own plain,
For life does go on.
I will not die
For I'll also come back
To say, 'Goodbye'
To the loved ones I'll leave behind
And forget the rest.

Cats Galore

In my back garden
Are many cats
That come from near and far
Ginger toms, albino's, and black ones
Enough to make you stir.
Neighbours they throw bricks.
I just throw some water.
Gardens, they have no pride in
As flowers get flung so far.
Cats are always arriving
Sometimes many more.
There may be two, even twenty four.
Oh, my poor garden grows
With such an effort.
I'm always in a state
No sooner have I planted
When darned cats galore appear.
New neighbours have moved in.
With, yes, one more,
But it's only a kitten.
So far, so good it seems.
We have a dog.
He's having endless fun
Chasing those darned cats.
I need not take him for a walk
Just let him loose in garden
To watch the cats run up a tree.
Fur flies; it's endless fun
To see the hackles rise
Along the backbone of our dog
As he jumps up on all fours.

My Dream Home

A white island villa
I plan to retire to,
Somewhere abroad;
So hot, so sunny,
Somewhere in the Caribbean
On an island
With warm friendly people
That greet you
With warmth,
Whitewashed walls, with red roses all around,
A few friendly chickens
That run from the rain.
My dog and I would be so happy
Living on an island in the sun.

My neighbours would be few
Away from the city
And the smells;
Shops will be basic,
Flowers in abundance,
Taxis don't hoot,
And the sea is so warm
Near my white island villa
In the sun.

Early Post

The postman used to come early
Now he is always late;
Some time ago he arrived at 8.
Now it is nearly three.
He seems to come now as he pleases.
The last arrived in car.
It used to be a regular sight
But my dog now is in disarray
As he never knows when to bark
For the free newspaper delivery
Or the printed circulars.
The parcel force van arrives when he can
So there is no routine anymore.
Just when it comes, you will know
For the dog might bark,
If he has not got fed up with waiting.
He used to lie by the door
Until the post landed on his back;
Now I guess he has given up
Same as myself.

Elvis Presley
(*The king is dead*)

He died in the Seventies
But remembered by many
For long after his death.
His Home is still open
As many flock to Gracelands
To see the King's house.
There have been many sightings
But no one is still sure,
As many fans lament, 'The king's alive and well'.
They have seen him.
Many have not.
Cars he may have had,
Women for certain,
But the cry goes out
'Long live the King'.
May his music go on
As his films are seen
Around the World;
And in Britain
His story will go on it seems
For evermore.
His memory will live on
As others fade away.

Eastertime

Easter is a day for celebration
As the Lord goes to his crucifixion.
Among the people and the donkeys
Is a man of immense power and giving.
He hung on the cross to forgive us our sins.
Mary worshipped at his feet as he hung there dying.
Other men said, 'Please can you forgive me?'
He reassured them that they would go to Heaven
To confess their sins
To behold a new joy
In the rising of the Lord
As the stone was rolled away.
Today we sing his praises
Now and for evermore;
The Lord *has* risen
To behold a new beginning,
To forgive our sins,
To make us humble
As we go on our merry way.

Festival

The celebrations that go on
In Rio, and in Edinburgh;
The Fringe and the drama,
The singing and the applause,
All through the night.
The merriment and the wine,
People smiling,
People crying
Through the tears of the clown,
Those that walk with stilts,
Those with big bold skirts,
The hula-hoops, and the skipping;
The castle and the tattoo
All around the world
At every chosen date
Is a festival of merriment and singing,
Of laughter and enjoyment
Until the early hours,
When, tucked up once again in bed
To start again
The next day.

War is Alive and Well

Saddam Hussein is out and about.
The guns of war are never alone
Sleep is nil
As you stay awake
Looking for a time-bomb
That will go off one day.
America is on the alert,
Britain too, never rests.
We are all on edge
As the machines roll around.
We hope it never comes
War, on all angles.
Life has no expectancy.
Death is a sure cry
From the joy of life and good
To the quiet of the grave
Where no man never stood.
Saddam is a danger
To all mankind.
Let us be rid of him now
For tomorrow never comes
Until he is dead and gone,
But not resting
In his grave.

Sail to Sea

We sail to sea over this vast ocean
To see what we will see,
Many islands,
Many people
In lands so far away.
We travel to small lands
Then on to big,
Through the sunsets
And the sunrise
And the music
Of the lands.
The people may be friendly
Or maybe they will be hostile,
but when we arrive
We will know
What will be
Will be.

Has Man Changed?

From caveman in the past
To man in all his glory,
From the pioneers of the Wild West
To the servants of our gender,
To see man as he was
And man as he is now,
With Mobile Phone and Computer.
It used to be a Time Machine
Like an H.G.Wells' science fiction;
Now it's just a toy
With fast cars as of now,
From push bikes and penny farthings,
From baggy trousers to just flairs,
From Renaissance to Victorian,
From Pompadour to the Wars.
Has man changed?
I guess he has,
But – my man has not
He's still a caveman at heart –
Bless him!

The Truth Will Out

In times of trouble and strife
With wars and medicines alike,
Saddam Hussein is an evil man,
But, alas,
The truth will out.
In times of anger and woe,
In times of justice and peace,
Bestowed upon the very few
The truth will out.
War can never last.
Happiness goes on.
Life is like a game of chess
Each man being a pawn.
Days of glory do go on.
Days of peace also.
In times of trouble and strife
The truth will out.

Here I Am

Here I am worshipping at your feet
To wash away sorrow,
To let in joy,
Breaking away the chains that hold me;
Giving beauty and leadership,
Honouring you, Lord,
As I am Raised up high
To meet you in Heaven,
Worship and praise.
You are light in darkness.
Power to you, O Lord.
You can break the chains that hold us down.
Your Sheep, O Lord,
That follow you.
Here I am to praise you
Now and forevermore.

I Had a Vision

I had a vision last night:
A piano, with an empty vase.
I knew you were gone.
It was a message from God.
The vision had dark curtains
But they let in the light
Through an open window.
I felt a great comfort
Knowing you were safe and sound.
I woke up, and the vision was there
On the bedroom wall.
I looked at it for a long time it seems,
Then it faded; I felt alone.
My empty heart,
My sad and empty heart.
But I felt a great comfort
Knowing you were with God,
Playing your songs
With a new and open heart.
My room was dark
But your vision was bright.
I will always love you
Until the day I die.

Obesity

Some are large
And some are fat,
Some are skinny,
Some mislead.
They are all fat in their own eyes
Making diets quite a fad.
Some do not need to lose weight
And some progress to losing pounds.
Many people are led astray
As new members join exclusive clubs.
Money is lost
And money is won.
Dieticians score many points
As in their book your weight is read.
Many people are obese with age
As weight goes on in middle-age spread.
'Keep your chin up,' you are told
As the diet works,
But not for many.
So keep up in spirit as the weight is lost
Go for the loss, and not the burn.

I Honour Your Love

In our hearts we honour you,
Receive your love
So good and whole;
The spirit within me
Cries out to you,
Receive your love
So good and whole;
Honour your love,
Praise your name.
Till the day we die
And join you in heaven
We honour your love.

The Mosquito

Little one,
Why do you bite me?
In seconds of our precious time
Blood you take.
Is quite often mine.
Pain is caused
But once your fill has been taken
Off you go to another shore.
Because of this
Your friends I swat
Quite happily with great gusto
As you hover around me.
The part you bite will itch continually.
So, little one,
Fly away
Off to another shore
Where you can bite quite happily
Another.

I Love Life the Most

I love life the most:
The smell of the earth,
The crisp green grass underfoot ,
The singing of the birds,
The call of the eagle,
Children playing,
Children crying,
Lovers that talk and cuddle,
The bark of dogs,
The crispness of the waterfall,
The cool clear water,
Perfume odours that pass me by,
The phone that never rings;
Apart from those cold callers
The voice that says 'Goodnight',
The voice that says 'Hello',
The scent of aftershave,
For my old car that never rusts,
The milkman who has time to talk
The postman who delivers my bills,
My husband as he never talks.
Ah, bliss!
For God created all this:
Our homes,
The bricks and mortar
And the landlord who talks
And talks.
Yes, I love life the most.

An Ordinary Soldier

He goes into the trenches,
Comes up to fire his rifle,
Sees his friends die around him
While he still lives
To see another day.
Tomorrow never comes.

Life goes on, so does the killing
Of boys and men;
Women and children left alone,
Families sad and tearful.
The news never ends
Of the massacre and the destruction
Of lives and buildings,
And the vicar knows the end will come
For he will lead the funerals
Of those brave men and boys who die
For their countries
And their families.

See the birds fly high above
As they survey the dead bodies below.
Blood is spilt, dead bullets that were fired.
The scent of death looms all around.
Tomorrow is another day,
But life goes on.
Who really cares?
Who will remember these heroes
As the years go on
And you and I depart this sodden Earth?

It Screams in My Mind

Love, you wronged me
And now you lost me;
You're just an illusion,
A figment of my mind and despair.
Once we were one,
Now we are incomplete.
It screams in my mind
Now you are gone.
Long live the memories
Of a great and lasting friendship,
Of a joy never to be seen again.
It screams in my mind
A lasting and restless night,
How you wronged me
And now you are gone.
Memories I only have
Of your smile and laughter,
The music and the noise.
The stage was set
For us to be just one;
But now it is just one,
For now, the present and the future.

Life's a Picture

Life's a picture
Of most ordinary things:
War fields,
Cemeteries,
Flowers in bloom,
Weddings and cremations.
The world is colourful
Made up of many things:
Of me and you,
Not black and white,
But in glorious colour;
Food is colourful
If you look at it right;
Words are also colourful
But not the swearing that goes on,
But a colourful repertoire
Of music and song.
Dance is magic.
Life's a picture
Of many things:
Of me and you,
Our homes,
Our hearts,
The gentle breeze around us,
Dogs that bark,
Cats that purr,
Babies crying,
And adults that bring joy,
Thanking everybody
For just being them.
The world is a wonderful place
Of many things:
Big and small.
What new venture we will find
When we wake up tomorrow
And see the world through our other eyes.

Loch Ness Monster

Nessie is her name.
She is an illusive creature.
Photos have been taken
For many now a year.
Some claimed to have seen her
But by now she must be thin,
Since time began
Talk has been of her.
She's somewhere around .
Maybe in the bushes.
Maybe now she's had children
And that is what we spy.
Maybe the original Nessie is now dead
Because it seems strange
That Nessie would still be alive
In the bracken and water of Scotland's Loch.
Still, she's been on T.V.
And that counts a lot.
Maybe one day I'll make a visit
To see the illusive Nessie.

Losing Weight
(A Slimmer's Dream)

Losing weight is a slimmer's dream
From 20 stone to 16.
Your looks re-organise themselves
And you have a great respect for yourself.
Slimming clubs are a big help
With encouragement along the way,
A pat on the back,
A shake of the hand.
The scales grimace at the start
Then swell with pride
As weight is lost.
Slimming drinks, foods are an aid
To losing weight along the way.
Exercise is a must,
From Skipping ropes to jogging.
Your teacher is your best friend.
Sometimes men can't understand
But you look good as the weight sheds.
Called a 'Fatty' from the start
But look at me now
As I walk down the street
Slim, petite,
And a head full of pride.

Missing You

We are missing you
Now that you have departed.
You have gone away from us,
You left without a word,
But peace is in our heart
As you write your news from afar
Telling us of your new country
And the peace it holds within your grasp.
We tell you that our country is at peace with yours.
Long may it continue,
Long may peace survive.
One day you may return full of stories
About the country you moved to,
About the country that lives for peace.
We tell you about the life over here,
How people try to help each other
By bringing peace within our island.
Hopefully no war will start in our lifetime
But the serenity of our countries
And the battle for ongoing peace will live
In our hearts
And in our prayers
In our churches
And in our schools.
Long may peace continue
As we bear the scars of life
Of the ups and downs
Of our age and of our kindred.
You may have long departed
But peace is in our hearts.

Obese Children

Children are heading to obesity
With chips, crisps and the unhealthy foods;
Some eat with common sense
But very few
Eat a proper lunch at school
Or at home.
Temptation is always there
As adverts bombard the children
With unhealthy living.
The Americans are the worst
With different sizes on their streets.
What a difference correct eating makes
With plenty of exercise along the way;
The gym is a start,
Swimming, too,
Walking the dog and jogging are very good
To stop the obese children
From early death
And an early grave.

Our Granddaughter

Today you are five.
We have sent you
Our present,
And a card.
It is a pop-up cake,
Pretty colours
With a badge.

Fifty miles away,
We have your photograph,
A tape of your voice,
A video of you dancing;
But today
The day is yours
And we await your visit.

Your five candles will burn today
On the cake
That your mother's baked.
So, little five year old,
We toast to you this birthday -
Many happy wishes
And a happy fulfilled year.

Peace Across the Waves

Let there be peace across the waves,
From Havering to Germany.
Let there be light
At the end of the tunnel,
The vision of harmony and understanding
Of goodwill and joy
To meet each other from across the waves
By plane or Sea
Or hitchhiking and backpacking;
To meet on foreign ground
Which is alien to the other,
But peaceful to the rest;
To say a fond 'hello'
And not a sad 'goodbye'.
Forever friends in peace,
Forever friends in harmony,
For many years we have been friends in peace
May it long continue
Until the day we die.

Pregnant Bumps

Oh, the joy of childbirth
From conception to the day
We have a tale to tell;
From small bumps to enlarged ones.
One birth, to sextuplets,
They all start small
But end up different sizes.
It also seems different shapes
As the child kicks around
From the day of man arousing us.
We feel, oh, so broody.
We crave for different meals
From extraordinary to the absurd,
Such as custard with pilchards
Or, banana with egg.
Thinking back, I'd say a big yuk
But at the time it was heavenly,
As our desperate spouses ran around for us.
But as soon as child is born
They, by magic, disappear;
Down to the pub, or football,
After all, it was nothing to do with them.
But, as women we all know
For nine months we are treated as queens
Until the day of birth;
Then, by magic
It's all gone.
Back to normal
Until the next time.

A Doctor's Lot

I sit in the surgery
Listening to soothing background music.
There are magazines in abundance,
White walls,
Linen suits;
To hear a sniff or a moan
Is the norm while waiting to be seen.
I'm only here for a check-up;
Others have dilemmas.
The overture will soon arrive:
'Mrs Hancock, Room 25'.
But, no, it does not come.
I wait it seems for ages.
My appointment was at 1.45;
It's now 5.30.
I'm getting tired and frazzled.
I want home;
To go to bed,
To nurse my cold,
To soothe my aching head.

Reflections of Life

Looking back to the past,
Was it so happy then?
Schoolwork, rejection, making friends
Wondered if it's lasted?
Seeing friends so old, but new,
Warms the heart through and through.
School photos of how we were,
But looking to the now
Were we fat, or were we thin
Long hair, short, are we still the same?
The names that we were called,
Some not repeatable for our ears,
How did we get those awful names?
From our so-called friends?
Being called 'E' was bad enough
But one was called 'Smelly'.
How she suffered every day
At the hands of her tormentor.
Many now have jobs and a family.
Some never did make it.
They died before reaching twenty three.
Many have moved home
On occasions, many times.
All we want is happiness
And to be young again.
So reflecting back on to life
I was happy then.
You knew where you stood with your friends.
Now the world is in such a mess.

Retribution

The dog was bought for a guard,
Tied up outside in a backyard,
Housed in a kennel that was too small
And every so often went to the park.

When boredom set in,
No toys, and no work,
One day it got loose
And went away,
But went quietly berserk.
The owner could not understand why it went that way
As it flattened him
And then bit his hand.

The police were called.
The dog was taken away.
The Rescue Society have now got him.
They were really annoyed.
The owners were scolded
And sent away
To be re-housed
In a dog's kennel.

September 11th 2002

One year on
And Ground Zero is formed
To the memory of those who lost their lives
In the Twin Towers massacre.
Bin Laden has never been found
And everyone is scared,
For one does not know if another attack is due
In England, or overseas
There will be services around the World
As we all re-live the pictures in newspapers
Of the cruel deaths those people endured.
We cried for hours.
We will cry again
Until those who destroyed are captured,
Never to put their evil to work ever again.
The New York skyline has now changed forever.
Will a fitting monument be built there
To commemorate the lost lives?
Will there ever be justice in the world
As silence around the world will fall
At the time the planes struck
Taking innocent lives?

I Love My Dog

I love my dog
For he is cute
At only six years old.
He is friendly and warm.
He has a black/white coat
And a warm wet nose
That gets this way
When he's excited and hot.
When he's calm
It's cold and dry,
Eating each bowl of food happily
And at play
Wagging his tail joyfully.
He hates black dogs.
The bigger they are the better.
But small dogs he gets on with
No matter what colour they are.
But black dogs he despises,
For what reason
I do not know
But there you are.
Like a human
He's also fussy
About whom he plays with
Whom he cuddles,
Especially when it's time for bed
And tomorrow's another day.

Sitting Examinations

Oh, the headaches,
Oh, the paperwork,
Oh, the teachers
Telling when you can start.
The clock on the wall goes slow.
Time drags as you study the words.
You long for a drink.
Your throat is dry.
You're feeling nervy.
Two-hour long examination.
Will you get an 'A' or a 'D'?
Maybe you will go to University.
Maybe you'll go to college.
Maybe you will rejoice at the results
Or maybe you will cry.
A certificate is all you need
To get to where you want to go.
Soon time will be up
Then the final answer you will know.

Something More

How can we be so rich,
When half the world is poor,
When we eat our fish & chips,
And crave for something more?

How can we be so blind
When all around can see,
To wash in clean clear water
And crave for something more?

How can we be so dim
When the world is Light
And people always long
For homes, and clean crisp linen?

Why then, are we healthy,
When half the world is unclean?
They long for clean clear water.
They long for good strong houses.
We crave for something more.

Let us join together
To bring the poor together,
To unite in their starvation,
So……..
They don't crave for something more.

Stand, Soldier of The Cross

Stand, Soldier of the Cross,
First-begotten from the dead
With your face to the rising sun,
With your robes well bled
And your anger gone.
Rise, ascend to Heaven,
Soldier of the Cross,
Drink the true and living water,
Eat the tasteless bread,
Turn wine into water,
Feed the many thousands,
Soldier of the Cross,
Though the lowest of the world
You will not be forgotten;
You will reign in true Majesty
So stand, Soldier of the Cross.

Dieting

Every day we're bombarded with diets
From one fad to another;
From books to magazines:
'Try the F-plan, or the B,
Try eating less, or anything you want.'
Articles are always in the papers:
'If you lose weight, you will feel better'.
The bank balance goes down
As you join clubs and associations;
Weight is lost there, in your purse,
But do the inches fall away?
Every day it's a treadmill,
Weights, and slimming drinks,
But are you losing anything -
Except the weight in your purse?

Such Love

Such love cries out in pain.
The love of Jesus is whole,
Wrapping his arms around each of us.
Such love cries out in pain.

He tends our every need.
The crucifix was love for us.
Such love deserves our love
And for bringing us together
Until we meet again.

Such love that we adore.
O Jesus, you have saved us
As a fountain of life.
You died for us
Upon the cross of Calvary.

Summer Storms

Once again, here comes the sun.
The mini tornados that sweep Britain:
The floods and the anguish;
For on our streets instead of cars
Are boats and rafts
Along with our possessions,
Sand bags that fill our summer days.
Where have the flowers all gone?
Very seldom see any birds
That used to sing until the dawn;
But instead, there is shouting,
Road rage and the swearing,
Floods along many rivers,
Torrential rain that soaks us.
We try to smile
To say 'Hello, have a nice day',
But some summers can be hard,
Others quite heavenly;
But those are very few.
Roll on the winter.
We'll have then a few snowmen
And, yes, floods again,
all over the country.
I long for a proper summer,
Plenty of sunbathing.
Where has it all gone?

Swing Wide the Gates

Swing wide the gates.
We enter our Heavenly King's presence,
Sitting by his feet
Mighty in victory;
Raised as whole
To rule the Earth in Majesty,
Until the day we join him.
Hallelujah to him,
Our Heavenly King!

The Cottage

In the countryside there is a cottage
With a thatched roof
That overlaps the windows.
The windows are small.
The garden is large
As many flowers grow around the cottage:
Hollyhocks, lupins and jasmine.
The scent is overpowering
As bumble bees make their mark.
Butterflies come over to dance around the flowers
As the bees make way for honey.
The garden gate has an archway
Of yellow roses and red.
It welcomes you with open arms
And tea is served at three.
Tables are laid out in the garden -
Tablecloths, napkins and tea.
Scones and jam make you feel hungry
As you survey the garden green.
The walk around the house is breathtaking.
Old furniture and new have their scents.
Breathing in the wood scents, and the yellow petals
Makes you feel heady and dizzy.
It's a joy to know the cottage is there,.
Deep in the woods where no man goes
It's in a dream, you see.

The End

One day soon our lives will be over.
When our day comes
Who will be there?
Who will sing our praises
For our time on Earth?
Who will give the service?
Who, indeed will be alive
When our time comes
To depart?
Not many will have a cathedral service,
Not many will be remembered,
But we all remain under one
planet, that is Earth.
We live and breathe on this fine world.
Every day we die.
Every day we're being born.
Every day a funeral.
One day it will be ours.
Until then we'll rejoice
And live our lives in full,
Until we depart this sodden Earth
And that will be –
THE END.

Samson

He is a Welsh Border Collie
Full of love and giving.
He now is twelve years of age
But still is going on one.
He loves his walks in the park,
Chasing everything in sight.
To come to heel is not too good
He has a mind of his own.
Black and white with brown eyes
And a white tip at the tail,
He bounds on his merry way
Making out that your not there.
A dog full of love and kindness.
He nuzzles you when you're not well
And barks at some unlikely times,
Until you say to him, 'Stop!'
He goes on his merry way
Leading his doggie dance.

The House on the Corner

There is a house
That will be gone
If the developers get their way,
For they need the space
To build some flats.
An eyesore, you could say.
We thought it was a listed building
But the council say, 'Be gone!'
To the house on the corner.
Your days are numbered and gone.
The house is growing weeds
Instead of pretty flowers.
The walls are crumbling.
The windows gone.
No frame, just a hole.
Front door has been boarded up
As cows and horses roam the grounds .
When the developers get their way
They will also go
No cows and horses,
No house,.
Just a block of flats.

Life Goes On

Our time on Earth is short
But in heaven, it is timeless.
We are only passing through on Earth.
God has other plans
We go to school, we have a job,
We don't know when we are called
To go to heaven;
Only God knows.
Many of our friends have gone
But we have happy memories
Of our lives with them,
Of their mutual trust,
So when we die
It will be a long journey,
Longer than the one we're on now,
Longer than time itself;
But God will protect the good on Earth
And the bad shall stay 'dead'.
So as long as you're kind
You'll have eternity
To live forever
In the presence of God.

Is There Nowhere On This Planet?

Is there nowhere on this planet
That we can live in peace?
Where people live in harmony
In every creed and race;
Where people smile and cuddle,
Where there is no famine,
Where love is all around us
In every creed and race?

Is there nowhere on this planet
Where we can dance and sing?
Where love is all around us
In everything we do;
Where joy comes into being
And evil is cast aside;
Where peacemakers come among us
And hold us side by side.

Is there nowhere on this planet
That life is true and kind;
Where war does not exist
And peace is all around?
Where gossip is not so rife
And the truth is always heard;
Lies, it seems, rule the day
Of a true and loving peace.

The Joy of Christmas Time

To see the young faces light up
As they open their presents one by one;
To hear the birdsong first thing in the morning
As the day begins to unfurl;
To put the turkey in the oven
As you count the people to cater for;
To wash down the meal with wine and a song;
A perfect carol to a perfect day,
Family come around,
Sleighbells ring out the old.
And welcome in the new;
Snow glistens on the ground
As children hurl a snowball at their friends
And miss you just about.
The happiness in people's hearts,
The chatter and the mistletoe,
The minstrel's song,
St. Paul's Cathedral's carols.
You sing along
As your heart soars above.
Christmas tree glistens with baubles and bells,
Presents for every person,
Young and old;
A sleep in the afternoon
As stomachs are full
And everyone cuddles you,
Because it is Christmas -
And a happy New Year to everyone!

On the Downbeat

Boys and girls come out to play,
Mozart sounds like Brittney Spears
So the children say
Taught in the playground about pop music
Confuses it with classics.
Why, oh, why?
Can the children hear?
Or, is it they are blind?
To the finer chords of music
That their parents sing?
Looks like a total mix-up
Between children and their friends,
Who hear the classics at the pop awards
And sing out-of-tune to all.
Ear-defenders are a must
As violins screech out a chord
To the sounds of Rainbow
And Atomic Kitten.
l long for a bit of peace.
Well, there's always the 'off' switch
On the radio.

The News in General

Open any paper,
And what do you find:
Murders, rapes and suicide,
Muggings and arbitration,
The Prime Minister's on holiday,
The Queen is out to lunch,
Parliament is now sitting
After a long earned rest;
Football players earn a fortune
As nurses complain about their lot.
Where is the good news we long to read?
There must be some,
Somewhere.
Crossword puzzles keep you alert
As you scratch your head for answers.
We look forward to tomorrow's paper
As good news is a 'must'.
Animal news can be amusing
Some of it is sad
As the hedgehogs get run over.
Foxes can be in the paper
As the farmer fires his rifle
Only to be arrested.
Tomorrow I shall write some good news.
Yes,
Tomorrow's another day.

The Postman Calls

He used to come twice a day
Now it's only once.
The post gets more.
The stamps go up.
They try to save
But lost quite a lot in savings.
They are in debt
Into millions, not pounds.
The customer always pays.
The queues grow out the door
They start early
But arrive at your house late.
Now they want £14,
For a second delivery.
Who are they kidding?
In the end there will be no respect
As post goes missing
And parcels get lost.
Where do they all end up?
Not in my hands.
As I crave for more
I guess next stop will be
To pick up your own post
From a box.
In my lifetime I hope not.
I'm still pleased to hear that thud
As post lands on the mat
From near and far.
Unwanted or urgently awaited.
Good news and bad
Every day at my door.

I'm Going on a Journey

I'm going on a journey
Now I've passed to the other side;
I see a path of stars
And pillars on either side;
I'm wearing a white robe
For Christ has chosen *me*.
I'm not simply destined to the 'other side'
But to a world of love.
I hope to return to my loved ones
To say a proper 'Goodbye'
And say to them 'Don't worry'
I'm going, but I hope
Won't be forgotten.
Not many loved me on Earth.
I was taken advantage of
But now I'm happy than I've ever been.
In the world on 'the other side'
I'm with an ocean of people
Who care, and keep me calm,
For there is no anger here,
Just joy, and a pillow for your head.
I've found new friends,
And I have a new heart.
It is bringing life to my old body
For I am changing fast.
New laughter, new spring to step,
For God is here.
I am happy

Fat Cats Sitting on the Fence

Fat cats sitting on the fence,
Fat cats licking up the cream
Of mice and men;
They take our profits
Bleed us dry
Until we squirm.

They know no bounds,
They tell no lies,
Just yearn for money;
Until the day they die
They pinch and pick
To enrich their pockets

Fat cats sitting on the fence;
One fell off, another tripped.
If they don't watch it
They all will fall;
We'll be rich,
They poor as mice.

So, fat cats, please take heed,
Watch every move you make;
We'll be watching
In your conservative houses,
In your rich state;
One day the bubble will burst
Then - no more cats.

One More Step

One more step I go with you
Around the World,
Around the Sun.
I walk in the shadows of my former self
But now I'm in the sun
Worshipping you, O Lord,
Praying your every word
Until one day I'll be with you,
To see your face
And to touch your hands
That were pierced with a nail,
To cherish your every word.

One more step closer to you.
Every day's a hurdle
Of life's up's and downs,
And no great comfort
except in the comfort of your word,
And one day a great exhalation
To see you,
To touch you.
So, one step closer to God I take.
My mind at rest
And worry no more.

The Student's Lament

I need to get a home
Some money and an income.
I've tried hard
But to no avail.
I've tapped into cash machines
The balance is quite a shock.
The rent man will come soon.
But a sweet and a hankie
Are all I possess.
My purse is quite empty.
My home the same
Or so it will be
If this goes on.
When the chips are stacked against you
You battle into the night
To face yet another day
Of doom and gloom
Along the way.

The Quest

We keep on searching for an answer
But find nothing,
But death, destruction around the world;
Living corpses that surround us,
Me, you and everyone,
Waiting for a bomb,
Waiting for an explosion,
Hijackings that go on,
Planes in sky that explode with innocent lives on board.
When will it all end?
The death, destruction to our planet that we call Earth.
The newspapers are full of it.
Gossip, traumas, and the occasional lie.
We all want to live in peace.
So, let's go on our quest
To find the peace and harmony we all crave.
Long live our quest
For harmony and peace.

Cure For Snoring

I hope one day there will be a cure for snoring
For when it comes, I'll be happy.
You see, most nights my husband snores,
So loud at times, it shakes the walls.
I long for defenders
But I'm afraid they'll slip
Down in my ears;
Hence, no return.
I prod him and I roll him
But to no avail are my efforts;
Still he snores up until he wakes,
Sometimes at four,
Other times eight.
I fall asleep during the day
But awake at night
When I should be asleep.
So, please can you help?
For I get no rest
From this grunting and a groaning.
There's even a foghorn noise from him.
If there is a cure I'll be glad .
I long for him to be cured
Amid all his noise.

The Waiting Game

Where there is time, there is patience.
Where there is good, there is evil.
Where two lives collide
In the space of a moment
There is the waiting game
Where love is lost and won;
Where peace and war collide,
Where we depart and leave ourselves
Behind in the space of time
There is, the waiting game.
You and I go on
To a moment in time where we remember
Lives are found and memories go on.
Will we see those people again or not?
There is the waiting game
Time is just a tick-tock of the clock.
Clouds reform above our heads,
Weather changes, and people leave
Buried beneath the soil, or cremated within walls.
Life is beginning, a child screams,
Waiting for what?
We will not know,
But the waiting game goes on,
Destiny - it's game of woe.

Weatherwise

The weather, how it twists and turns,
One day thunder, next day sun,
Mini tornados that career around Britain;
Even swells that come from the sea.
We take out our umbrellas in the rain
Until there's a strong wind
And umbrella's turn inside out .
Oh, where's the sun?
The summer's of the 1960s
Lots of ice cream?
Now it's global warming.
We know not how our days will be;
Rain one day,
Sun maybe the next,
Maybe a thunderstorm
Maybe lightning.
Oh, the weather, how it twists and turns.
You cannot rely on the weatherman,
Just your own prediction
On each and every day.

The World, The Universe

The World is round
With many countries;
Some big, some small
Some just in-between,
With many islands
Around the globe,
Many people
With many tongues,
Many animals
In far flung lands;
Some big,
Some small,
Some so tiny
You need a microscope.
But you and I
Live on this vast planet
With many friends
And many enemies,
So many
That we extend
Into the universe
Into maybe another dimension in time
Where we evolve
Until the end of time,
And our planet collides
And explodes with the moon,
Blown into oblivion,
Blown into the universe
To evolve in some far off shore
In another land.

Unsung Heroes

There are people upon this planet
Who are never known
For all their acts of kindness,
Which are often vandalised.
They go around in silence
And receive no applause
For they are the spectators
Of this frozen world.

On this orb we call the world
There are stars which lift us
In a spiritual way.
Why the world is so appalling
I will never know.

There are bright stars oozing talent.
There are quiet ones in disarray
Like an icon of creation.
We go our separate ways.
On life's stage we perform
With humility and flair
Like a great creation,
But still remain
anonymous.

Your Ghost

You stood in the room,
A smile,
A friendly smile,
A big Cheshire grin
To say, 'I love you'
In all my dreams
You came back.

You died a few months ago
You went to heaven
And God sent you back.
You had to see me.
I could not make your funeral.
Your family phoned
To say how sorry they were,
But I knew you were safe.
I knew you were in no pain
But happy in heaven
With your friends.

You said 'Take care'.
I said I would.
Your smile, your tears,
A passing whisper
A happy smile.
Your family phoned.
I could not make the funeral
But I know we'll meet again
In heaven, with God.

The following books, by Elaine Day, have been published by Feather Books:

"Prayer for Jesus and Other Poems".
ISBN 1 84175 028 X £4.00

"A History of Havering".
ISBN 1 84175 230 4 £6.50

"Closer to Heaven".
ISBN 1 84175 227 4 £6.50

"Knocking on Heaven's Door".
ISBN 1 84175 223 1 £6.50

"Poetry Comes Like Waves".
ISBN 1 84175 233 9 £6.50

"All Year Long".
ISBN 1 84175 247 9 £6.50